MONKEY RANCH

MONKEY RANCH

Poems by

Julie Bruck

Brick Books

Library and Archives Canada Cataloguing in Publication

Bruck, Julie, 1957-
    Monkey ranch / Julie Bruck.

Poems.
ISBN 978-1-926829-74-6

    I. Title.

PS8553.R8225M66 2012   C811'.54   C2011-908121-0

We acknowledge the Canada Council for the Arts, the Government
of Canada through the Canada Book Fund, and the Ontario Arts
Council for their support of our publishing program.

   Canada

The cover image is a detail from *Cookie...waiting,*
by Donald Roller Wilson.

The sections are divided by monkey fingerprints.

The author photograph is by Kara Schleunes.

The book is set in Sabon and Fontin.

Design and layout by Alan Siu.

Printed and bound by Sunville Printco Inc.

Brick Books
431 Boler Road, Box 20081
London, Ontario N6K 4G6

www.brickbooks.ca

This book is for Lewis

A life should leave
deep tracks...
It should abrade.

         – Kay Ryan

Sort of, said the monkey merchant.

         – Russell Edson

CONTENTS

I

II

III

IV

V

I

This Morning, After an Execution at San Quentin

My husband said he felt human again
after days of stomach flu, made himself French toast,
then lay down again to be sure.

I took our daughter to the zoo,
where she stood on small flowered legs, transfixed by the drone
of the howler monkey,
a sound more retch than howl.

Singing monkey, my girl says.
She is well-rested. We all are. As we slept, cold spring air arrived,
blown from the Bay where San Quentin
casts its sharp light.

Tonight, my girl will tell her father
(a man restored, even grateful, for a day or so) about what she
saw in the raised cage.
Monkey singing, she will tell him,

and later, tell every corner of her cool dark room,
until the crib springs ease because she's run out of joy,
and fallen asleep on her knees.

Why I Don't Pick Up the Phone

Because it's the school nurse
saying one child has written
on another child and the ink washed
off but the writing remains:
We can't read it, but you'd
better get down here
right now and do something.
Because someone is in a locked ward
for their own protection, meaning
someone else had to commit them,
and now walks around with a heart
like a hammered anvil.
Or, another has fallen and even though
you're next of kin, you're too
far away to catch or comfort.
I do not lift the headset; sift
instead what's coming as the tide
sorts its affairs. What washes
up should bear signs of who
it carries, like an eyelash stuck
to the edge of a stamp—and no, smartass,
I don't mean caller ID. If I can't
have the living glance of the guy
from Western Union when he hands over
the onionskin, then just give me
two minutes more at the window, kids
from the daycare returning to their ark,
clinging to their red rope like little
shipwreck survivors, before I pick up
and let the world name names.

Snapshot at Uxmal, 1972

Leaning into the sun-warmed stone, she must
be fifty, still beautiful, her strong frame
easy inside her loose shirt and jeans.

He's gone to a larger ruin for the day,
someplace deeper in the jungle, more
challenging to reach by jeep or tank.

Here, where the early Mayans worshipped
the sun, appeased their gods with routine
live sacrifice, she will photograph only

small details in black and white. Later,
he'll describe the jungle's colours, ornate
bird plumage, the vast scale of what he saw.

She will need the afternoon to document a single
weed growing through a crack in the pediment,
a candy wrapper blown against an ancient step.

And there is the daughter, fifteen and not
quite as sullen as she's going to be, shouldering
the pack of lenses, her mother's fine-grain film.

Her father's impatience hasn't flared in her yet,
though she carries that too, an unstruck match,
trailing her mother through the tall, dry grass.

Maison Vendu

St. Sauveur-des-Monts, Québec

Jiggle the key and the door
will unstick, bright red enamel
giving way with a satisfying pock.

The air between the two
doors is liquefied sunlight,
drowsy with flies, amniotic.

A row of coat pegs above
a pine bench, a straw hat.
The smell of old sails.

Rest here, between
outer and inner doors, full
sun honeying your bones.

No more agents in SUVs,
or transfers or titles.
No strangers in the kitchen.

They say the weather's turned cooler.
Soon leaves will cover the house.
Then snow.

The vestibule always held
the day's heat, so stay as long
as possible, be a fly in amber,

and take a vestige of this
with you when you go,
a slice of fifty summers

you'd wrap up if you could,
tight, in waxed paper,
for the road.

At the Music Concourse

Someone took his life last night,
on a green park bench and lies,
this many hours later, under
a cracked yellow tarp, over there.
The morning sky swells
with barely withheld rain.
Chinese music fizzes
from a boom-box for Tai Chi
by the fountain, while tourists
wander past, museum-bound.
A child bangs a ziploc bag
of oranges against her thigh,
until her father loses patience
and takes it away. Her protest
is brief, muted as the police officers
drinking coffee beside the white
coroner's van, while workers
scour the bandshell's facade
with high-pressure hoses.
In this thickened atmosphere,
an ascending jet sounds louder
than it should, and at least one
leashed dog sits, nose skyward,
tracking the noise like a meerkat.
Little changed overnight except
weather, a low front off the Pacific.
The only colours: strung police-line
and a small potted ginkgo,
its little fans the hammered gold
they turn at the cusp of winter—
trembling, though there is no wind.

Love to, But

Our very important neighbour is
fused to his new Cingular headset:
now he can talk *and* walk.
Blah-blah-blah goes Mr. de Broff.
This makes it hard to hear
even the packs of feral dogs
howling all night, or the cats
doing what they do in our dark
fog-bound city gardens.
The world needs its chemistry
checked, that's for sure.
The poisoned river is high,
fast at this time of year.
Fences between houses are down,
and we all like our boundaries.
Pharmacies? Closed.
All essential services, shut.
Time to fetch my daughter
from a birthday party which
ended in 1963, but she runs late.
Sometimes, I have to pry her
from the door jamb, carry
her to the car like a small,
warm totem pole with sneakers.
A yellow Hummer slipped
through a crack in our street
on Tuesday: not seen nor
heard from since, despite
the crowd of looky-loo's
still milling around out there.

Love to. But these are
strange times. I could
expire before I meet
you at the gate. Yessir.
Love to. Toothache.
Can't.

The Mandrill's Gaze

Foraging among the zoo's shrubs,
he glances up periodically, plants
his psychedelic rump and takes our measure.

Above his Bastille Day snout, the mandrill's
hazel eyes are small, deep-set, and when
he fixes them on yours, I dare you,

turn away. He bears the same expression
children have, small children who
must accept the hand that's offered

with neither trust nor suspicion—look,
the zoo is full of them today, lurching
up and down the popcorn-strewn paths,

leashed to their larger ones, their eyes
full of knowing that wherever they're headed
with their short legs, their inadequate steps,

they've been taken by the hand.

The Change

So, I've done what my body was made for.
My eight-year-old is all legs, careening
down the basketball court, and I do

acknowledge the pulls and pushes of tides,
moons, of love and such, even if I stop short
at crystals and meet-the-plankton music.

My husband hums in the house,
my daughter sings while she plays.
I'm hunched at the kitchen table,

jaw clenched, staring down a blank
grocery list when that stringy mouse,
the one who holds keys to this place,

scrabbles across the awful linoleum
for the first time today and my shriek
is so sudden and muscular and primal

I know I've pulled something in my neck.
If this new Tin Cat™ does its job, I swear
I'll carry the jumpy, humane contraption

straight to the park in my bathrobe,
calmly raise the metal lid and let
the mouse go with a kind, steady hand.

I'll be better than I am,
pretend to love
this creature I'd rather drown.

*What does it mean to love
the life we've been given?*

Elizabeth Bishop's Room

*Adapted from an unattributed YouTube
video tour of Bishop's childhood home,
Great Village, Nova Scotia*

See how the skylight's been
shimmed in place by a pair
of snub-nosed scissors.

These aren't the original
pair but a later,
replacement pair.

I suspect the well-worn
flowered linoleum
dates from her time.

Such a tiny room!
It's impossible
to photograph it properly.

I can only get
bits and pieces:
the cabinet

and its latches.
*An immense, sibilant,
glistening loneliness—*

The narrow bed
pressed
under the eaves.

Gold Coin

Two weeks past Chinese New Year, red
paper children and dragons still drape
the copy shops and nail parlours.
I wheel the baby through the street's bright offer.
She hoots and points her articulate,
fat finger: comic books, pantyhose,
Beard trim $4.50, and the Chinese name
for a certain kind of orange, *Gum Chin Chang,*
posted above the fruit like a musical score.

What gives this day such perfect pitch,
a held note against the usual desolations?
The baby laughs—there's a white moon up there—
as we rattle west with the hand-me-down stroller.
A new girl in town and her mother (new
too on this particular morning), we're rinsed
with sunlight and wind off the Bay, glossy
as the scarlet envelopes you can buy here
by the pound and stuff with money,
meaning luck.

Milk Teeth

She wants to trade them
at the standard fairy rate
and grow new ones, their edges
serrated as a steak knife's.

She wants them out like Hannah's,
the tall girl at kindergarten, who cries
into her mother's raincoat until she's
promised a call, "the minute I get to L.A."

She tests each stubborn vestige
of baby-self with a finger, craves
to plumb sweet and sour crevices
with her tongue, to taste

her own blood, which we've tried
to contain in that small body,
calling it protection. She wants
them out now. And all that comes after.

The Trick

Blinking in the half-light, almost bright
after the school's dim corridors, we'd pass
the line of poplars, tall black sentries
at the outer limits of the playfield.
Streetlights flicked on, one at a time,
new snow coming down, heavy and wet.
We ran the hill and slid, our boots
etching serpentines on the snowy sidewalk.
A big boulevard to cross, then the empty
lot, whose Scotch pines knelt beneath
the snow's accumulation, blue in this light,
before the final, dangerous curve.
We always sensed them, but were never
prepared for the three or four boys
crouched between the blind flanks
of houses, coiled to grab our hats and run
with impossible suddenness, schoolbags slung
like ammo belts across their 8-year-old chests.
We jammed the hats our mothers bought
deep in our pockets like charms—anything
to deflect their rough attentions,
though I knew it meant they liked us:
I had two brothers and understood
to love meant to torment.
A schoolmate's mother who sang
in a barbershop quartet
had already hung herself at home.
Another child's father would soon seal
his garage door with duct tape
and start the family car.
She left no note, his would say
he loved them all. I thought the trick
was to sidestep even the smallest emergencies,

disappear in our blue or gray duffel coats,
hats clamped in our wet fists, to will
them by like fire engines when the fire
is elsewhere and much more urgent—until
they'd blown past, their boisterous voices
receding, their three or four *Canadiens* jackets
drawing so close to the vanishing point,
you could hide them by holding up a thumb.
We'd walk home quietly in the softly
falling snow, small monks who remained,
to all appearances, untouched.

A Marriage

His paintings were small, suggestions
of houses, pinpricks of green for trees.
She'd set her glass down, say, *Paint*
like you're blind, from memory and passion—
two words he especially didn't care for.
She'd say, *Paint like you're on fire.*
But their house was already burning,
and he was going blind *and* deaf.
So he'd carry the painting back down
to the basement, resume with
his thinnest sable brush. He would
never touch her the way she wanted,
though she kept asking him to,
like this, in front of everybody.

Entre Chien et Loup

My father stands inside the front door,
waiting for my mother, who's changing
in the bedroom with her door shut because
she can't stand the feel of him waiting.
His hot breath, she calls it, *that airport look.*
It is winter dusk, the hour when solid things
grow indistinct, a confusion of dog and wolf.
My father is grey with impatience.
Where they're going isn't clear—probably
a party—nor whether they're actually late.
My mother had appeared ready to go,
but now her clothes struggle on the bed.
She roots through the closet for something
to make her more beautiful.
My father won't notice her transformation
—what the hell is taking so long?
She knows this, but wants him to wait
exactly where he's standing
—Aww, for chrissake, can we go?—
where he's stood for over forty years.
Perhaps she is dressing for a man at the party,
perhaps she is dressing for her own pleasure.
She is *getting dressed* and will not
be rushed. She discounts a second garment,
is now inside the closet, admiring
the finish on a third.
Any minute, my father will storm from the house,
start the car and sit with the motor running,
exhaust from the tailpipe staining the snow.
In twenty years, he will leave my mother
for someone who's already waiting for him.
My mother will enjoy tonight more than he does,
take longer to leave the party than he'd like.

At the door, he'll joke with the host
and hostess—*Wasps leave without saying goodbye.*
Jews say goodbye without leaving.
My father will march ahead to the car, while
my mother takes her own sweet time on the icy walk,
holding the hem of her long red coat.
Unless she's still curled in her pantyhose
and bra, hugging her knees in the closet.
The carpet is rough against her skin.
She used to be in retail, loves well-made
clothes, loves the idea of well-made clothes.
She buries her face in a blue silk robe,
tears taking her by surprise—*God*
dammit!—He has shut off the car, stomped
back inside, rattling the house, aftershocks.
From the open front door, a smell of exhaust.
The waning light finds my father in the hall,
melted snow pooled around his overshoes.
Deep in my mother's closet, a small bulb
snaps on, casts a warm circle
where her neck meets the shoulder.
When he's left her, her days will mimic
these nights before parties. Details will
derail her, destinations overwhelm. But tonight,
she's his problem, and he has stained her snow.
And there's still enough light to see by.

New, Used, & Rare

Darling, asks the elderly lady with bright
red hair, *where have you hidden Used Cooking?*
It's November, the time of afternoon when people
often come in to get out of the wind.

B-2, points the pierced clerk, *below*
Drinks and Smokes. You're a dear, she says
and shuffles in that general direction,
confiding in whoever is listening:

My sister's in assisted living. Thursdays,
they bake soda crackers with butter and sugar,
add chocolate chips and bake a bit longer.
My sister says you'd never guess

they were Saltines. I want that exact
recipe—perhaps a book on candy.
A thin man with purple skin lesions,
leaning hard against Used Film, looks up

from his book. *Maybe you should visit*
your sister on a Thursday, he suggests.
Behind the register, the clerk checks
his watch against the store clock's time.

Sweetie, she says, *my sister's in Delaware.*
They are moving past Used Poetry, closing in
on Travel Lit: *Honey*, says the frail man, *we can*
leave right now. Darlin', let's drive all night.

Goodwill

On his knees, the new employee adds more
black shoes to the black shoes rack.
His manager floats by in a leopard muumuu,
says, *Good job, Johnny. When you're done,
your shift's up, so punch out for today.*
He raises his face to each customer, says
Sir or *M'am*, offers help which no-one takes,
his face wide and eager as a child's.
It's a new job: to arrange black shoes
which smell like people's feet, to offer
unsolicited assistance, and to like it.
This first day has gone very well, indeed.

Missing Jerry Tang

It's been over a year since he was last seen
near the park's boathouse, where birdwatchers
congregate for coffee and small children lob
oversized chunks of stale bread at the ducks,
igniting and re-igniting their squabble.

Fluorescent flyers—*Missing husband and father*
of two, 40 years old, seizure disorder—
have been replaced with more recent sightings:
pictures of the two blue herons who nest here,
an egret teetering on its fragile orange legs.

His children go to school with ours, his wife
tends her patients at the hospital on the hill.
The man who ran the coffee stand died suddenly
last fall, but the place has been reopened
by a new man who looks uncannily like the original.

It was raining, windy, when a groundskeeper
last saw someone who looked like Jerry—alone
on a bench, he said. He appeared to be weeping.
The man gave him an umbrella and left.
He has black hair and brown eyes—

The regulars are grateful for their coffee,
to reclaim benches as the sun strengthens
past the winter solstice. The turtles also
line up on their island, drinking in the light.
White-gold wedding band worn on left hand,

inside engraved with initials and date—
The park's naturalist gathers her middle-school
flock, trains their binoculars to the heron nest.
She teaches each child how to list for posterity,
and to date their findings in a log.

Please

Send them all home, these frail containers:
Barack Obama's chiselled skull and my husband's
round one; my brother's grey brush,
and our braided girl, her sweet wake
of green-apple shampoo. Keep them inside:
the matriarch's white waves, pink scalp
showing through, and this morning's student,
blue streaks above her midterm on compassion.
I want to say, *Duck, stop, that's high enough,
cover your heads, haven't you heard?*
Look at the baby's little bald coin
where she rubs against her sheet;
or the "bright, engaged" kid who will shoot
his classmates and himself soon enough,
his freshly-buzzed cut as he smiles
for the high-school photographer.
Lin, as her hair grows back and she gels
those defiant spikes, and Otto's warm, fuzzy
dome, small enough to cup in one hand.
There's my platinum Auntie, ingénue at 80.
Paul at 18, centre part, gold to his shoulders,
sometimes pulled back with a rawhide cord.
I'd reach down the years, say, *Paul, you'll
leave four children, don't start that car.*
But he's restoring a piano, sweeps hair
from his eyes as he places ivory inlay,
his head always dusted with powdered Steinway.
Now, Mrs. Bhutto's, on its slender, patrician stalk.
Silk, loosely tied around her hair,
one dark wisp, blown free.
I saw this at noon, on the BBC.

Common Goods

At first, no-one notices the ancient woman reach
for diet root beer in Aisle Three, straining
the lurex dice woven into her sweater.

Nyet, nyet! shrieks her greying daughter,
as short arms windmill for the top shelf,
No root beer, nyet, doctor, nyet!

Gnarled as a shrub, *matryoshka* is sending roots
deep into the vinyl steppe of Beverages,
calling all shoppers to see five durable feet

of Russian history, each finger gold-ringed,
a century past the Revolution, martyrs and poets,
past glasnost and the endless, cold oceans.

She digs in the heels of her sensible shoes,
extends ten manicured fingers—*nyet!*—and holds
fast her ground—until the younger woman shrugs,

makes the Russian sound for disgust, extracts
a six-pack of root beer and, holding it high
above the empty shopping cart, lets it fall.

Should You Ask

Coffee must be strong enough
to stand a spoon up in.
The death penalty is wrong.
Babies should nap outdoors
in a shady spot, under a tree.
The Blue Angels' dissection
of the sky is cruel to psychotic people
and not good for anyone else.
Sometimes, when the traffic evaporates,
for a minute, this is the 19th-century.
Soup demands bread.
The smell of a child bringing
fresh air and exertion indoors is the best.
We've become more fearful
but history repeats itself: perhaps
we're no more afraid than we were
when we conked each other with clubs.
Old friends are best friends.
Richard Thompson is a guitar god.
Leaving one country for another is hard.
The purpose of a prenatal class is to give people
the illusion that they are in charge.
Poetry is, as Szymborska says,
The revenge of a mortal hand.
There is no grand design when someone
dies—no comfort to be found there.
I stole that phrase from Adrienne Rich.
Oh well. She took it from Dr. Williams.
Philip Larkin was a great poet.
Great artists are not the same as angels.
Jasmine at night is a drug.
It is good there are still old people

on their stoops to comment on the passing parade,
how sometimes people stop to speak kindly
with them about the Giants and whatnot.
A clean desk isn't hard to achieve
unless you are a child, in which case
it could be impossible.
My parents will live forever
despite mounting evidence to the contrary.
There are more students out there
like Ka-leung, who will do anything
to distinguish the words *kiss* and *kids;*
I would sit with him forever,
hissing and spitting those sounds.
Toxic cleansers smell good.
Permanent markers, even better.
No socks with sandals.
Shame is the most difficult feeling,
bar none.
Laughter is always good
except when you have to pee.
Sunflowers really are wise, which
tempers the sting of the summer's end.
As adults, we're asked
to accept the endings
woven into our DNA.
Spoons will stand up straight
before that happens.

Scientists Say

After Neruda

Deep in the seabed,
when the Twin Towers fell,
two enormous tremors
rocked the eels
of Jamaica Bay, Queens.
A small disturbance
under the great water,
quickly settled. Now
they lie like circles
of the earth again,
mating and devouring,
dressed in ritual mud.

A School Night in February

In his attic bedroom, a teenaged boy
watches his lava lamp's colours implode.
Downstairs, his mother has burned
her wrist on the oven rack: she's
tired, distracted by an earlier incident
to which we are not privy—
as she is not privy to the basement
location, behind the furnace, under
a tarp, where her son has stored
the rifle he will carry to school
via torn hockey bag and lift—
with a steady hand, a witness will say—
from under his grandfather's old black coat,
sleet still clinging to the shoulders.
Tomorrow night, all night, in tidy,
heavily-mortgaged homes like this one,
lamps will cast angled windows on the worn
suburban snow, sixty miles west of Chicago.
Seen from a distance, say, a moving train,
it will appear that every other house
has left lights on for a weary traveller—
someone expected much earlier, someone
who must have been inexplicably delayed.

Mutanabbi Street, Baghdad

On a pile of bricks, someone had left a pink plastic
flower, a pair of glasses, and a book with crisp, white
pages. They glowed in the black debris of Mutanabbi Street.
This is his shoe! a man cried out, *I bought it for him.*
It was Friday, 9:06 a.m. The man was slim, with peppery hair
and square, grey-tinted glasses. He clutched a black chunk
of leather melted by the heat. *I bought it for him.*
He kissed the piece of leather, placed it gently
next to the flower, the eyeglasses and the book.
Come and see it, he yelled to five men carefully
digging through debris. *It's his size.*
This is your shoe, he yelled to the pale blue sky.
My son, I bought it for you. The six men, all relatives,
were hunting for a teenager's remains. The boy had been
shopping for notebooks on Mutanabbi Street, named
for a 10th-century poet. They had been digging since
Wednesday, morning till night. The men stared blankly
at the shoe. No-one had the heart to speak, so they kept
digging. *Don't step so hard,* the father said.
Don't harm him.

Newsreel

San Francisco, 1918

"The war is over and into Market Street pour
the men and woman of the city, ready to celebrate.
Up and down the street they parade, delirious
with joy, for some of them have come to know
the meaning of war. Grotesque in their
influenza masks, the people of San Francisco
celebrate. You've seen the signs they carry:
Kaiser Wilhelm is Sweet William Now.
Who's Afraid of the Huns? Some are
signs of hate, while most are outpourings
of a great joy, for this day, November 11, 1918,
marks the end of an era of bloodshed
and violence, and the beginning of peace
and good will on earth. And those who have died
have died to make the world safe for democracy,
they've swept to victory in the war to end war. And so,
San Francisco celebrates in 1918, because
the war is over, and there'll never be another."

After Wildfire

In the brand-new house, one of two
left intact in the subdivision,
the dog startles at every sound.

Nothing's been touched:
paintings, books, a worn favourite chair,
a carton of milk on a counter.

The once-suburban streets are emptied,
familiar names heat-fused to their poles.
The lots look smaller without houses,

without the shadows of their trees.
The dog interrogates the room, while someone
kicks an empty can along the sidewalk.

After the bulldozers, a moose
came to drink from the swimming pool,
a few dazed raccoons, the velvet mole.

Now an engine turns over, a truck
moves out, leaving its trace
on the almost-evening air. Wait—

Across the ashy, lunar lawns, with
their particulates of melted siding, come
troops of tiny white mushrooms, from spores.

Live News Feed

I am watching my mother's neighbourhood
explode on live TV, when Ruth, my father's
girlfriend, calls from her renovated kitchen,
reports she is baking an apple cake.

On screen, one more disaffected youth
in a trenchcoat, and bodies—trauma units
filling up fast with the dead and injured.
My father is 92, she is ten years younger.

They live in her B.C. apple orchard
after a twenty-five-year affair, which
somehow slipped under everyone's radar,
lasting half of my parents' marriage.

Are you watching the news? I ask.
Yes, she says, *terrible isn't it?*
If I'd been able to speak, I would
have said, *Yes Ruth, I haven't reached*

my mother: perhaps she's dead.
But my father needs to talk
about an insight he's gleaned
from a Steinbeck novel-on-tape.

I ask whether he's seen the news.
Awful, isn't it? he says,
and returns to *East of Eden.*
It is already dark in Montreal.

Blue police lights bounce on wet
streets and buildings I knew better

than my own hand, everything
cordoned with yellow crime-tape.

Once, I'd thought we'd all driven
my father away: conversation at the family
table was fast, digression the rule.
He'd often dozed off by dessert.

Guns drawn, a SWAT team flanks
the door to my mother's building.
My father wraps up Steinbeck, inquires after
my health, says their kitchen smells good:

Ruth took those apples from the neighbour's orchard.
She swears stolen apples have more flavour.

Islands

At certain times of afternoon, the only
ones left are couples like that one, seated close
to the bistro's sliding windows, paused in their talk.

The lunch rush ended hours ago, set-up for dinner
hasn't begun, and the waiters eating at a booth
in back are only too happy to look away.

These two look a little damp, like
a sudden wave had washed over them.
Perhaps they've been crying.

A palsied man shuffles past the window,
drool swinging from his chin; the street
steams after rain. Certain afternoons

are islands. Then empty cabs start
to rattle the avenues, angling for fares,
straining for the tunnels, the bridges.

Monkey Ranch

Our monkeys were striped
green and yellow, except
for the red and white ones.
Outside the house, a screaming
kaleidoscope of stripes chased
stripes, until they settled
in the branches at dusk,
to pick each other's nits.

Father tired of monkey
farming, took a job in town.
We starved our monkeys.
Day by day, they slowed,
and when I picture them now,
or dream of how it was,
they stagger in the black
and white of old newsreels.

It took them a whole year
to die off while we watched.
In those days, children did
as they were told, and Mother
always favored chinchillas.
But they used to wear such
cute little monkey hats—
red, white, yellow, and green.

Cold Cases, Adult Division

They're everywhere and nowhere—a man
leaves his wife and children, the morning
like any other, after making phone inquiries
about private piano lessons, and appears
to have been sucked from the face of the earth.
Someone's sister plays a gig in rural Nebraska,
walks from the club to her car, carrying
her guitar case, ten—or was it fifteen
years ago? *Cold*, say the police, *maybe
gone of their own adult volition*,
their families left haunted by a spectral
outline, like the suggestion on the skyline
of an old hotel, right after it implodes.
This week the weather turned colder,
but one park vagrant still wears
his shorts and singlet, both the colour of dirt.
He's draped himself in an old wool blanket
which gives him the weight of a weathered sage.
Or would, if we could stand to look at him
the way our children do, when they're still
too young to strip the world of miracles.

Once

Once, I wanted a particular man
to wake and touch me so badly,
I vacuumed the bedroom while he slept.
The harder I hoovered, the deeper
I wanted him, the more I hoovered,
the deeper his sleep. The more
he slept, the deeper my wanting.
It had yet to occur to me that
a man who sleeps while being
hoovered is not a wanting man.
It took much hoovering to drown
out that small complication,
which made me want and hoover
for another desolate pre-dawn hour
a man who did not want nor wake.

Indécis

In the absence of faith, indecision is
the mind's great stay against death.
— Benjamin Constant

Chicken or shrimp,
sell or keep,
cerulean or indigo,
go, stay?
Duck or goose,
how much,
how soon.
Paper or plastic,
how tight,
how hard?
Closets bulge
with painful shoes.
Rugs stacked so
deep they ripple,
making it hard
for a person
to stand.
The air
palpitates, can't
breathe itself.
The worried air
needs rest.
Chairs
to the ceiling
and nowhere to sit.
The world
drums
its fingers.

How to Be Alone

Night-time is for sleeping, we'd chant
to set the clock, to relax her fisted hold
on the crib bars, the minute terry-bound feet
testing their new purchase on the mattress.
We were teaching independence, self-soothing,
how to be alone. If that fails, the book
advised, *There is no more today,* a phrase
so thick with terror, it took hold immediately.
Baby slipped off the ledge and we stood by.
She sank into the dark without a cry.

Girl in the Yellow Cardigan

A mother shouldn't do it, shouldn't
watch her girl on the crowded playground
from the high library windows, the only
new kid at middle school, edging
groups which form and reform with each
incoming surge of backpacks and bodies.
A mother shouldn't witness her clutch
that neon green container, which she'd
begged to forgo today (so she could slip
lunch inside her book bag), and which
I'd insisted she take to *keep things cold*.

On the schoolyard, she holds it stiffly,
away from her body like an outdated purse
with its short, awkward handle, a contagion.
No, a mother must see this—the mother
who, on this very first morning, prevailed
because here's what mattered: the thing
is insulated, has a special compartment
for its little block of cold, blue ice.

My Father's Clothes

He wore a sheared lamb winter hat
from Russia until it disintegrated.
But the rest of his wardrobe never
took his shape. Navy sports coats
with brass buttons, grey business
suits—as pristine at day's end
as when he first slipped them on.
He could have been a dressmaker's dummy.

No one taught him touch, not his critical
parents in their Panama hats, custom
couture and alligator shoes, not the icy
Czech nurse who bathed the boys year-round
in Long Island Sound. No one showed him
how to live in his clothes, how an elbow
needs to worry its way through a sweater
like the nub of a spring bulb, poking
finally, through the rank, wet earth.

He never pressed his shape on any of us—
only his uprightness, intention, his need
to be going, the Russian hat riding
his head like a black fur envelope.
And when he grasped his children
in affection, say, fingers around the back
of a neck, he always squeezed until it hurt,
and we could only pull away, leaving
his bewildered hand groping for a pocket,
and finding it basted shut.

Boy At The Window

Let's just say he fell because
he was up there in the middle
of the night, prying the damn
thing open with his fingers
from the outside, his taut body
filling the frame. Let's say
you panicked when you woke
with his shadow on the bed,
that you swore, rapped hard
on the glass with a travel
umbrella that just happened
to be lying on the nightstand.
That you didn't tell anyone
there'd been an incident,
or glance down to see if a boy
lay crumpled in the courtyard,
or had returned to the shadows
that produced him. You did
not look for this boy's mother:
he shouldn't have been at the window.
You're a mother of daughters,
and cannot be trusted with sons.

The Help

Polished brass doorknobs, retrieved
newspapers, vegetables, mail, meat,
new clothes from that day's ads.
They carried in thick glass jars
of yogurt, and sweating bottles
of Guaranteed milk, left between
back doors with a handwritten note,
correct change. Planted annuals,
deadheaded perennials, weeded lawns,
watered all. Raised children, waxed
floors, starched shirts, poured
milk, filled pools. Baked cake.
Scrubbed toilets, washed curtains,
beat rugs, ironed sheets, aired rooms,
fed dogs, cleaned silver, waited
table, scraped plates. Every night,
a checked apron, discreetly folded
on a shelf in the tidy kitchen
closet, before the last one out,
in thin wool coat and worn overshoes,
climbed the snowy hill to catch the #66,
support hose, work slippers, school
pictures of her nephews, and a book
of paper bus tickets to last
through the month, deep
in a shopping bag from Harrods.

Final Season

Family Day, Bay Meadows Racetrack, 2007

Every ten minutes the indoor arcades swell
with the roar of men losing the rent.
Small kids queue for an Easter egg hunt,
their pastel line threading between wizened
regulars, who've stepped outside to smoke
and wince, Racing Forms held against the sun.
Four more weeks of bright silks unspooling
but the place feels tarnished with retrospect.
A jockey walks by with his fly-weight saddle,
his face the colour of veal, as monitors
stream the fifth live from Santa Anita.
We watch the horses fuss and sidle
to the gate—each a gleaming ton of coiled
muscle—and in this slim window, our
forearms pressed to the singing rail, know
the exuberant, thundering release.

Today's Handicap

Comments from the San Francisco Chronicle's daily horse-racing stats.

Beat up on maidens.
May never look back.
Dull one.
No clue.
Can run with these.
Capable if fired.
Bred to be quick.
Hard one.
Lacks tactical speed.
Out of his gourd.
Been chasing better.
Back with own type.
Good heat.
Has best jock.
Best is needed.
Hung up in lane.
Never made a move.
Nothing yet.
Drops off.
Beaten favorite.
Knocking at the door.
Has won on the lawn.
Can't be overlooked.
View from afar.
In clever hands.
Cheap but honest.
Can't recommend.
Hits rock bottom.
Must do more.
May forget to stop.

The Winningest Jockey

He could hold that assumed prayer position,
be plucked gently as a lifted cricket from
the foam-slicked, heaving winner of this race,
its nostrils blown, and be lowered to the next.
So go the days. At season's end, a long bath,
his pose unfurling like a Magic Sponge™
until he walks upright, and we lose his sparse,
red hair to the parking lot—a bowlegged
slip of a man, moving from one sun-struck chassis
to the next, mumbling, searching for his truck.

Eggs Roll,

says the misprint on the Chinese delivery menu.
We're waiting for *Cashews Chicken*,
at play on the hardwood floor, since eggs
roll half-way across this living-room,
then arc in a wholly new direction,
again and again and so on. Since
the '89 earthquake knocked this building
from its moorings, an egg can't
rest, which could be what keeps
the shoe from coming home to roost,
a chicken from the door, or another wolf
from crashing down, since none of us,
crazed as marbles, can stop describing
the ground on which we too roll, never ceasing,
though we tire of it often and deeply.

The Wooden Family

They've stood on my mother's desk
forever, and now she wants me
to take the Danish family of five,
plus cat and dog. Smooth '50s teak,
they're featureless, simple shapes,
the kind that can trouble small children,
since they lack eyes, noses and mouths.
The mother has a little hole
in her chest where her infant
rests—the baby's removable,
leaves a cashew-like dent.
Also, a father and two more
children in descending sizes,
a mirror image of our own
former unit. I say, *no,*
no more tchochkes,
perhaps not gently enough,
and I'm jolted by her pained
stare, then ashamed.
But I hate that family,
its "good" design, and bogus,
Henry Moore solidity—
how even the slightest breeze
from an open window can scatter
them all, the smallest pieces
bouncing across her desk
before they hit the floor.
There must be some
absence, deep inside
the grain: all you have to do
is look at them sideways,
and they fly off in every direction.
Including the cat and dog.

Spoon

Knife has a blade,
fork has tines, but
spoon is most
dishy, receptive.
Soon, its peer group
will sharpen spoon's edges,
though this has taken longer
than experts anticipated.
Now might be a provident
time to stop giving
one to the baby.
Think, *substitute*.
But if you acquire
your spoon early enough,
before peer pressures
roughen it up, spoon
may also improve
satellite reception,
when attached at an angle
to a very small roof.

Girl in Her Brothers' Bedrooms

Since she shouldn't be up here,
here she is, older brothers away at college,
their musk still territorial. She drifts
between rooms, igniting the dust-motes
in diagonal shafts of winter light.

Their closets secret Elvis scrapbooks,
complete stamps of Borneo with wax-paper
hinges frail as insect wings, jars
of uncirculated silver dollars. She pockets
some to spend, but that's not why she sifts

the gun-metal desk drawers, inhales
their rich peat of eraser and pencil stubs.
Called to eat, she takes the stairs by twos,
holding in mind her return ticket to the smoothed
chenille, the water-stained maple night-tables,

to the drop in the belly as she stands
on the thresholds of her brothers' rooms.
Old enough not to climb back down, she's
still too young to jump. An unfinished letter.
A subway token. A dime. That vertigo.

Great White, Released

Yesterday, he circled the million-gallon tank,
bumping his snout on the turns. Around,
above the schools of silver-plated tuna
went the dented face—a solitary, endless
infinitive that couldn't hold a crowd.

Visitors moved on to the half-ton
sunfish, a pocked, prehistoric boulder
rolling its perennially alarmed eyes,
the grimace pure German Expressionism.
Children shrieked into their parents' legs
while the shark continued his autistic
revolutions, dull skin glancing off the glass.

Forewarned, we'd have watched
from our motel window today,
as the clustered biologists eased him
from their boat before dawn.
But when the vessel listed to slip
the shark from its sling, we were asleep,
saw the sure trajectory of a dorsal fin
only on the scarlet linings of our eyelids, where
a Great White swam straight for the horizon,
drilled his worn-eraser head down, and disappeared.

We woke to still waters, a single boat
rocking slightly, and five yellow-slickered
figures staring at the vanishing point, like
those airport workers who herald the big jets
out to the runways with their fluorescent,
hand-held cones, and restore them to the air.

Men at Work

I said, "Do you speak-a my language?"
He just smiled and gave me a Vegemite sandwich.
                    – Men at Work, "Down Under"

We middle-aged sense them immediately:
four brittle pop stars sprawled across
the rigid fibreglass chairs at the airport gate.
It's not just that they're Australian, that gorgeous
thunking English, or the stacked electric-guitar cases
draped with black leather jackets, or their deep
tans on this Sunday night in midwinter Toronto
holding everyone's attention, drawn as we are,
pale filings to their pull. Even their rail-thin
lassitude attracts us, as it must Doug, the portly
Air Canada gate manager in his personalized jacket,
who arrives to greet the band, cranking hands
and cracking jokes. Doug, who must live in
Mississauga with the wife and a couple of kids,
and who insists the boys come back to play Toronto
next year, when we clutchers of boarding passes
will have abandoned our carry-ons for tickets
to a midsized arena and a resurrected band
whose lyrics, though they never did make sense,
are laced to a beat that won't let go—now
propelling us down the carpeted ramps
of late-night flights on feeder airlines, hips
back in charge of our strange young bodies,
now shaking down runways in rows.

Dead Air

Today's phone-in topic was public art
and its social role, but the dispirited
caller had given up graffiti, since
she didn't believe in spray cans
and *never found the right felt-tip marker.*
My old desk radio was turning
into one of Dali's clocks.
Surely this voice was clinically
depressed before it lost faith
in aerosols. It sat on the ear,
the air, like a slab of bad cheese.
The pushy English host and her guests
were exchanging nervous glances, audible
from the shifts of their ergonomic chairs,
such imperative to lose this woman
without apparent cruelty, fast.
Someone must have fumbled for the right
switch, the digital heave-ho, the polite
sidestep, *so glad you brought that up—*
and missed: what followed was ten
seconds of Line Two's sad breathing:
This is how a person who can't paint,
someone with a hook in the heart, sounds.
Here is the wind whistling through
that particular canyon. And it's live.

Election Night with Dog

It bites, still pees in the house,
barks at every change, pulls
against the leash as if it just located
someone unsniffed since high school.

But when the young senator from Illinois
was declared President-elect, our child
watched, cross-legged on hardwood, weeping
for joy, the scruffy new dog in her lap.

It smells very bad when wet.
As she listened, it licked and licked
her streaked face, while she ran
both hands rhythmically down its spine,

head to tail, head to tail, and
then, for a second, I saw
the aisles of cracked sidewalk
down which these two can travel:

A girl of strong feeling, and her
crazy dog, on a long, loose leash.

Ocean Ridge

I used to watch my supple mother
bend to collect shells on the beach.
They piled up on the porch furniture—
she rarely threw anything back.
Look at how the water's made
a Henry Moore hole in this one,
she'd say, *look*—but I didn't want
to be told what to look at, how to see,
didn't want her using my head as
a spare room for her own, a self-
storage unit, though I couldn't have
said so then, not even to myself.
Instead, I'd get a knot in my chest
that tightened on cue, I'd darken.
Now, when I gaze at my daughter,
she raises her eyes to mine in defiance:
Stop looking at me, she'll growl, and why
am I surprised? I was looking at her brave brow,
the profile that's her own and no-one else's,
because yes, she's a physical extension
of her father and me—I'm looking at what
we made, and she knows this in her marrow, puts
on her 100-yard stare and turns her face away:
all I can see is the tip of one ear,
sunlit almost to transparency,
its delicate runnels and inlets
shaped as if by water.

The "World-Famous" Lipizzaners

They trail the trademark Royal Lipizzans,
a day or three later, eschewing big arenas
named after software for more questionable,
outdoor venues, county fairs like this,
where you wander among pygmy goats at dusk
to locate the gate, always pay cash.
There are fewer white stallions here,
and they don't jump as high, but the crowd
of fat men, angular women, and their sleepy,
sun-kissed kids cheers wildly and stomps
its boots in time to brave Beethoven squeezed
from two tiny speakers. *That's the way,
Santa Rosa,* barks the commentator
in his iridescent blue suit, a decade
or two past Vegas. *These horses
love it when you make a lot of noise!*
So do the red-uniformed women riders,
who grin resolutely through *quadrilles,
caprioles* and *airs above the ground,*
broadcasting their teeth. Best of all,
these horses like to jiggle from the ring,
halt, then bolt breakneck for the barn—
whee! Hang the rules! A stud stampede
of Royal Riding School truants! Oh less
than venerable Viennese, elbows pumping
their horny white stallions barnward
at suicidal speeds, driving Santa
Rosa mad with glee, as mushroom clouds
of dust ascend under the klieg lights,
coating our throats! Get a load of how
they do this in California, oh Emperor
Franz Josef, oh Elisabeth, mournful
Empress, oh Troy Tinker of the blue neon
suit! We eat this dust, we yell for more.

The Greater Good

With a truck, I could move that.
Open a restaurant. Or practice medicine.
I'd try harder, and if I tried harder
could move that without a truck.
This would leave less of a footprint.
And my own feet might widen
with use, creating steady
platforms on which to perambulate,
to see what needs seeing to, on
behalf of those who need to be seen.
How badly they need to be seen,
the unseen ones, and heard and,
sometimes, touched. Hell, I need
a truck. With a truck, everything
would be much improved. Won't
you buy me a truck? I could
provide a dog to ride shotgun,
muzzle wedged at the window,
one who alternates between
biting at and smiling into
the oncoming wind, who airs
his piebald gums to the delight
of all those we pass or who pass:
a most excellent truck and corresponding
dog, on the road to the greater good.

NOTES

"Maison Vendu" is for Nina Bruck.
"Love to But" is for Jeanne Marie Beaumont.
"The Winningest Jockey" is for Russell Baze.

"The Change": the last two lines are stolen from
Suzanne Buffam's wonderful poem, "Enough."

"Elizabeth Bishop's Room": the lines in italics come
from Bishop's prose memoir, *In The Village*.

"Mutanabbi Street, Baghdad" is adapted from a
Washington Post story by Sudarsan Raghavan. This
historic center of the literary and intellectual community
in Baghdad was destroyed by a car bomb in 2007.

"Newsreel, San Francisco, 1918" is adapted from
San Francisco Celebrates VE Day 1918, a film in the
Shaping San Francisco Series, The Pralinger Archive.

ACKNOWLEDGEMENTS

Thanks to the publications in which versions of these poems first appear:

Able Muse: "Once"
Eleven Eleven: "Monkey Ranch"; "Common Goods"; "Please"
Literary Mama: "How to Be Alone"
Maisonneuve: "The Winningest Jockey"; "A School Night In February"; "The Help"
The Malahat Review: "After Wildfire"; "Girl in Her Brothers' Bedrooms"; "The Greater Good"
The New Yorker: "The 'World-Famous' Lipizzaners"; "Men at Work"; "A Marriage"
Ploughshares: "This Morning, After an Execution at San Quentin"; "Missing Jerry Tang"
Rattle: "Love to But"
Valparaiso Poetry Review: "Snapshot at Uxmal, 1972"
The Walrus: "The Trick"

Al-Mutanabbi Street Starts Here, Beau Beausoleil and Deema Shehabi, eds. (PM Press, 2012): "Mutanabbi Street, Baghdad"

The Textual Life of Airports, Christopher Schaberg, ed. (Continuum, 2011): "Men at Work"

Three Poems, limited edition broadside by Abby Letteri (Dog's Tail Press, Wellington, New Zealand): "Gold Coin"; "How to Be Alone"; "Milk Teeth"

"Mutanabbi Street, Baghdad" was also printed by The Al-Mutanabbi Street Coalition in a limited edition broadside by Carol Todaro, as part of *Al Mutanabbi Street Starts Here,* a large broadside collection, digitized at the Jaffe Center for Book Arts website. These collaborative broadsides have been shown worldwide, with proceeds going to Doctors Without Borders, and a complete set will be donated to the Iraq National Library and Archive in Baghdad.

I am grateful to the Canada Council for the Arts; to Elizabeth Perry, John Donoghue, and Joel Yanofsky, who helped me untangle the manuscript; and to the buoyant crew at Brick Books, especially Alayna Munce, Maureen Harris, Cheryl Dipede, Alan Siu, and Kitty Lewis.

The cover painting is a detail from *Cookie...waiting*, by Donald Roller Wilson. More of DRW's work can be seen at donaldrollerwilson.com. By generous permission of both the artist, and the collection of Patricia Altschul.

*J*ulie Bruck is the author of two previous books, *The End of Travel* (1999), and *The Woman Downstairs* (1993). Her recent work has appeared in *The New Yorker, Ploughshares, Literary Mama, Maisonneuve, The Malahat Review, Valparaiso Poetry Review* and *The Walrus*, among other publications. A Montreal native, she lives in San Francisco with her husband and daughter, and two enormous, geriatric goldfish.